GREAT WESTERN
STEAM AROUND BRISTOL

COLIN L. WILLIAMS

D. BRADFORD BARTON LIMITED

Frontispiece: 'Castle' Class No. 5074 *Hampden* with an eastbound Paddington express leaving the eastern portal of the Severn Tunnel, 18 September 1957. Some four and a half miles long, this is the longest underwater rail tunnel anywhere in the world. Forming the principal rail link from England to South Wales, the tunnel was opened to regular service in 1886 after many engineering difficulties. Quite apart from the direct South Wales-London route, it linked Bristol and the West Country with the Principality and reinforced Bristol's acknowledged position as the hub of the GWR system.

Brick-lined throughout and with a generous bore inherited from broad gauge days, the tunnel requires a continuous maintenance programme. Single line working on weekdays, plus total engineers' occupation on Sundays, is a regular feature; the scissors crossover visible here is to facilitate wrong line working.

[T. E. Williams]

© Copyright D. Bradford Barton Ltd ISBN 085153 2527

Published by Enterprise Transport Books Ltd
3 Barnsway, Kings Langley, Hertfordshire WD4 9PW

Printed and bound in Great Britain by BPC Hazell Books Ltd

introduction

Bristol has always held an important position in Great Western history as the hub of its system, being a major route centre both in national geographical terms and in the development of the entire railway system in the West of England. Initially Temple Meads was the terminus of Brunel's original line from London, as well as the onward link to Exeter. Connection to Gloucester, Birmingham and the north, via the spreading tentacles of the Midland Railway, came in the mid-1850s, with ownership of the station becoming a joint affair between the two companies. A rail link westward from Bristol to South Wales, to replace the centuries-old service by packet steamer, was depen-

dent on a somewhat unreliable ferry crossing of the Severn but nevertheless this new link across the wide waters of the estuary generated additional traffic. The opening of the Severn Tunnel in 1887, a massive feat of civil engineering for its day, forged the main South Wales link—indeed the traffic this brought caused congestion that threatened to overwhelm the main railway network in Bristol until the opening of the Badminton direct South Wales-Paddington lines early this century.

Congestion at Temple Meads was a major drawback almost from the completion of the first platforms there. As passenger traffic grew, both long distance and on local journeys, the inadequacies of Temple Meads became readily apparent, and even more markedly so with the growth of holiday traffic to the West Country, particularly in the years after the First World War. Cramped stations and their environs in the major cities were perhaps always a failing on the part of the Great Western, it might be said. However, in 1929, as one of the various Government-sponsored schemes designed to cut back the heavy unemployment then existing, a major reconstruction of Temple Meads was planned. Basically this involved a remodelling of the station—largely unchanged since 1877 apart from something of a rebuild when the broad gauge disappeared—including additional platforms and the lengthening of existing ones, considerable extra siding accommodation (more particularly for coaching stock) and additional running lines over much of the route from Filton Junction through almost to Bedminster. The opportunity was taken of changing also to colour light signalling in this central area: Bath Road locomotive shed was also rebuilt and enlarged. This extensive programme of work was completed by the end of 1935 and vastly improved the flow of traffic, yet without spoiling the external appearance of Brunel's original building. By this date, Temple Meads was handling a very considerable volume of traffic, over 150 trains a day both starting and leaving, as well as more than the same number again passing through, with a station stop. Many of these, moreover, changed locomotives, or involved the attaching or detaching of additional stock to or from the train.

Joint GWR/LMSR ownership, under GWR day-to-day control, continued to Nationalisation, when Western Region took over responsibility for all lines in the Bristol area.

In addition to Temple Meads, this volume covers an area from Pilning and Yate on the north side of Bristol, to Box Tunnel in the east: and to Ashton on the south side.

'Castle' Class No. 5013 *Abergavenny Castle* going well on the climb out of the Severn Tunnel on 9 May 1958 with the 12.05 p.m. Milford Haven to Paddington. [M. Mensing]

A freight eases to a stop on the down relief road at the east side of the tunnel, behind 42XX 2-8-0T No. 4289, 28 September 1959. Overtaking on the main is a 41XX Class Prairie which will halt and then set back to act as pilot engine through to Severn Tunnel Junction. Piloting of freights through 'the Big Hole' was customary in steam days, to cope with the steep (1 in 90/100) climbs involved and to ensure the minimum possible length of time this long single block was occupied. [M. Mensing]

One of the Severn Tunnel Junction pilots, 41XX Class 2-6-2T No. 4119, helps another 42XX Class with a freight up the 1 in 100 gradient towards Pilning, 9 May 1958. To relieve pressure of traffic through the tunnel at busy times, many loose-coupled freights were routed via Chepstow and Gloucester, particularly in the era of heavy coal traffic, when there was a constant flow of loaded trains eastward.

[M. Mensing]

As an alternative to the vehicle ferries plying across the tidal waters of the Severn from Aust to Beachley, the GWR offered a car-carrier service through the tunnel, operating between Severn Tunnel Junction and Pilning. Here, 51XX Class No. 4156 is at the former station with the usual 'consist' of end-loading bogie flats and a composite coach, 6 April 1964. The opening of the new suspension bridge two years later put an end to this car-train service which had originally been started in 1924. Still surviving today is another speciality of the tunnel, the fire-fighting train, composed of former milk tank wagons converted to supply water hoses carried on other wagons ready to tackle any train or similar fire.

[W. L. Underhay]

11

The car carrier train dropping down to the 'English' portal behind No. 4159 in June 1963, passing No. 6845 *Paviland Grange* with a parcels train. [T. W. Nicholls]

Apart from the few years when Cardiff (Canton) had a string of 'Britannia' Pacifics, 'Castles' were the normal motive power on all the main expresses through the tunnel. No. 5013 *Abergavenny Castle,* from Swansea (Landore), has an assorted rake of vintage coaches making up her ten-coach load, with a holiday season Saturday relief in July 1953.

[R. K. Evans]

With a clear stack, 'Britannia' Pacific No. 70016 *Ariel* with the 7.30 a.m. ex-Pembroke Dock makes light work of the uphill section through the long shallow cutting towards Pilning, September 1959.   [M. Mensing]   **13**

2-8-0 No. 3837 gets the signal for the loop as it approaches Stoke Gifford yard from Westerleigh, 27 February 1965. The line through Badminton to Wootton Bassett, opened in 1903, avoided the bottleneck and congestion of Bristol itself as well as giving a faster direct route to and from South Wales.   [T. W. Nicholls]

No. 5923 *Colston Hall*, from Cardiff (Canton), passing Patchway with a seven-coach semi-fast amid winter snows. [R. J. Leonard]

No. 6918 *Sandon Hall*, with a Cardiff to Weston-Super-Mare train, passing Cattybrook brickworks on the climb to Patchway Tunnel, July 1963. [T. W. Nicholls]

Another of the Landore 'Castles', No. 7018 *Dryslwyn Castle*, has the six mile climb behind her up from the 144′ depth within the tunnel, as she enters Patchway, 28 October 1951. After a level mile or so here, there is nothing worse than 1 in 300 on the fast run to Badminton and Swindon. The train is the 6.10 a.m. Fishguard to Paddington, loaded to the 14 maximum permitted for 'Castles' on this route.   [R. J. Leonard]

No. 7028 *Cadbury Castle* with a down express for West Wales in the cutting near Winterbourne, in August 1951. The long run down from Badminton through Chipping Sodbury saw some fast running by the Welsh 'Castles', right down to the tunnel, and speeds up to ninety were not uncommon. Holiday traffic to the various destinations west of Carmarthen, including Tenby, Neyland and Milford Haven, was a valuable source of holiday traffic each season, although never as important as that to Cornwall.

[R. J. Leonard]

No. 4968 *Shotton Hall* on 12 May 1951 approaching Patchway with a morning Swansea-Bristol train. She is on the new section of up line opened in 1887 which diverges from the older and more severely graded (up to 1 in 68) of the down line.

[R. J. Leonard]

No. 6862 *Derwent Grange* on the 1 in 75 climb towards Horfield and Filton Junction on the northern outskirts of Bristol with an Ilfracombe-Wolverhampton extra, 17 August 1963. Quadrupling of the tracks here was carried out in the mid-1930s.

[W. L. Underhay]

The fireman's view from the footplate of No. 1017 *County of Hereford* approaching Horfield, 30 August 1961. Approaching is a 'Castle' battling up the gradient with an overload.

[W. L. Underhay]

No. 6841 *Marlas Grange* at the head of an up empty stock and parcels train passing through Horfield in August 1963. The station here was opened in 1927. [W. L. Underhay]

Summer Saturdays saw every available mixed traffic locomotive pressed into passenger service to cope with the demands of the timetable; No. 6957 *Norcliffe Hall,* at Horfield, August 1963, with the 9.40 a.m. Carmarthen to Weston-Super-Mare.   [W. L. Underhay]

A good twelve-coach load for No. 6836 *Estevarney Grange,* from Penzance shed, working back home to the West Country with the 9.05 a.m. Manchester-Plymouth. Note the sand drag on the up line beyond the train.
[W. L. Underhay]

No. 4970 *Sketty Hall* approaching Yate Junction to the north of Bristol on the main line to Gloucester and the Midlands jointly shared with the LMSR, 29 July 1961. The train is the second part of the 8.55 a.m. Wolverhampton-Paignton. Below, No. 6930 *Aldersay Hall*, later the same day, with another holiday relief, from West Bromwich for Paignton.

[W. L. Underhay]

No. 5942 *Doldowlod Hall* with a freight near Yate, 29 December 1951.   [R. J. Leonard]

From Yate, a branch ran west to Thornbury. No. 9769 is passing one of the intermediate stations on this branch, Iron Acton, with a special on 26 September 1959. Subsequently the branch was closed and the track lifted but it has since been relaid as far as Tytherington to convey train loads of stone from the quarries there. [G. F. Bannister]

25

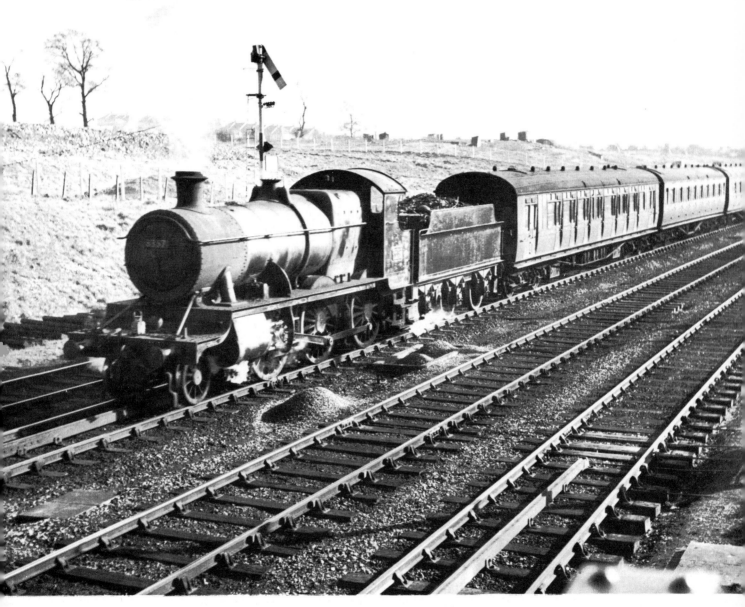

0-6-2T No. 6689, from Severn Tunnel Junction shed, lays a heavy smoke trail across the houses bordering the lines near Ashley Hill as it labours up the 1 in 75 with a long string of coal empties, December 1954.
                                                                    [R. J. Leonard]   27

Pannier tank No. 3702, coupled to a 'Toad', running quietly down the bank at Ashley Hill on a summer day in 1963.   [T. W. Nicholls]

'The Cornishman' (10.30 a.m. Penzance-Wolverhampton) on the steep climb up towards Fishponds, 6 August 1953. Helping No. 1004 *County of Somerset* at the rear of the twelve-coach train is an unidentified banker, providing assistance on this two mile stretch of 1 in 69/97 out of Temple Meads. [R. J. Leonard]

Two scenes at Lawrence Hill, where the ex-GWR metals go under those of the former Midland, *en route* to Gloucester; left, 'Castle' Class No. 5061 *Earl of Birkenhead* heading towards Dr. Day's Bridge Junction and Temple Meads, with a Cardiff-Brighton express, 24 June 1961. Opposite, No. 5976 *Ashwicke Hall* on the up fast line with a Paignton-Manchester train, passing beneath a Class 4F-hauled freight on the LMS line.

[W. L. Underhay]

Stapleton Road station in August 1963, with No. 7032 Denbigh castle on the 8 a.m. Wolverhampton-Minehead.

[W. L. Underhay]

The principal express between Bristol and the Metropolis was 'The Bristolian', introduced in 1935 and covering the 118 miles non-stop in 105 minutes. Here the up train, behind No. 7019 *Fowey Castle*, roars through Filton Junction where it starts the long fast run to Swindon and Paddington, 19 May 1959. Being a Friday, the load has been increased by one coach above the normal seven—still well within the capabilities of the later 'Castles' which vied with the 'Kings' on this service. [D. H. Ballantyne]

No. 7032 *Denbigh Castle* backing empty stock into the carriage sidings at Dr. Day's Bridge Junction, 24 August 1963.

[T. W. Nicholls]

Nominally designed at Swindon but looking as alien as only the smaller BR Standards could, Class 3 2-6-2T No. 82037, shedded at Yeovil, seen at Lawrence Hill with a four coach local from Severn Beach, 24 June 1961. Western Region footplate and shed crews took to the smaller post-Nationalisation locomotives quite well, recognising that they were efficient and easily serviced.

[W. L. Underhay]

Named expresses entering Temple Meads; above, No. 5011 *Tintagel Castle* with the up 'Cornishman', 27 April 1954 [T. E. Williams] and below No. 6015 *King Richard III* coasting in with the down 'Bristolian', 27 August 1954.

[D. H. Ballantyne]

Just taken over from an LM Region Class 5, No. 7029 *Clun Castle* waits to leave Temple Meads with the south-bound 'Devonian' on 26 September 1958. This express ran through from Bradford to Paignton and Kingswear. No. 7029, now well known as a result of preservation, was shedded at Newton Abbot and regarded as one of the best of the class.
[J. R. Besley]

Another view of No. 4903 *Ashley Hall* starting from No. 5 Platform at Temple Meads with the same Weston-Super-Mare train. Beyond can be seen Bath Road locomotive shed which in steam days was extremely busy, with upwards of 100 engines allocated there. 270 movements of light engines to and from the shed in the course of an average twenty-four hour period made the engine road by No. 1 Platform an enthusiasts' paradise.

[M. Mensing]

The west end of Temple Meads on a busy August Bank Holiday Saturday in 1956; No. 4903 *Astley Hall* waiting to leave for Weston-Super-Mare with a down relief and No. 5991 *Gresham Hall* entering with an up express. [M. Mensing]

Colour light 'searchlight' signalling at Temple Meads dates from the major re-construction of the station and its environs in the early 1930s. Two large power boxes—one at each end of the station—replaced a considerable number of manual ones, in a scheme that was part of the GWR's relief of unemployment programme, sponsored by the Government. Here, 'Castle' Class No. 5044 *Earl of Dunraven* is departing from the east end of the station with an up express from Weston. [M. Mensing]

It seemed to be GWR practice to give each of its areas of suburban operation a distinctive locomotive class—the 61XXs in London, the later series of 51XXs in Birmingham, 56XXs in Cardiff. Bristol's speciality was the later (4575) series of the 45XX class with larger sloping-topped tanks than the first series. This photograph of Nos. 5540 and 5546 with local trains at Temple Meads shows a scene still totally Great Western in rolling stock on 4 August 1957.

[P. J. Shoesmith]

A few words of commendation from passengers to the crew of No. 7024 *Powis Castle* after arrival at Platform 5 with the last down 'Bristolian' hauled by steam, 12 June 1959. Leaving Paddington at 9.45 a.m., the train was due in at 10.30 but—as the station clock shows—there is five minutes in hand. The ability for fast running of 'Castles' on this crack service rivalled that of the 'Kings'.

[D. H. Ballantyne]

Sporting express headlamps but in fact merely on station pilot duties, 57XX Class 0-6-0PT No. 3676 waits to draw vans from the rear of a recently arrived Plymouth-Manchester parcels train, 9 May 1958. This is on the up middle road between the main Platform 9 on the left and Platform 7. Beyond can be seen the overall arched span roof with its graceful curves which is such a feature of Temple Meads.   [M. Mensing]

A two-coach stopping train from the Cheddar Valley, just arrived at Temple Meads, 27 July 1963, headed by 0-6-0PT No. 3735. The station dealt with 150 passenger trains a day, starting or terminating there, in the pre-war years, and as many again passed through. Reconstruction work extended over a period of several years (1930-35), greatly improving the efficiency of what was one of the busiest stations in the country. New platforms and extensions to others, plus additional through lines, put an end to the congestion that had made Temple Meads notorious at times. [South Devon Railway Museum]

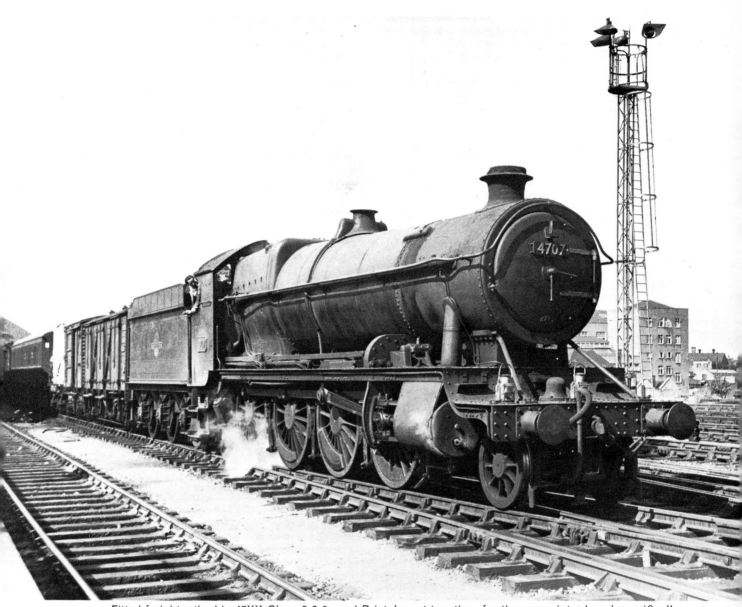

Fitted freights, the big 47XX Class 2-8-0s and Bristol went together, for they were introduced specifically for fast main line work of this nature to and from the West of England. A couple were shedded at St. Philips Marsh in the 1950s although Old Oak was their principal home. Here, No. 4707 waits with a train for the west, 22 July 1963.   [South Devon Railway Museum]

A sign of the times at Temple Meads, 9 April 1952, with the 11.15 a.m. Paddington to Weston-Super-Mare, 'The Merchant Venturer', headed by one of Western Region's two gas turbines, No. 18100. This pair were regular visitors to Bristol during their intermittent periods of service in the 1950s. They were powerful, but ugly and unreliable. Few would say its appearance could be in any way compared with No. 6875 *Hindford Grange* (opposite), also with 'The Merchant Venturer' headboard up, on 31 May 1952. She is coming off Bath Road shed to take over the train and work it on to Weston.

[R. J. Leonard/T. E. Williams]

Arrivals and departures; No. 5024 *Carew Castle* leaving Temple Meads with the westbound 'Devonian' in August 1956, and (below) 'County' Class No. 1013 *County of Dorset* coming round the curve into the station with a down express.

[M. Mensing/M. Jackson]

Night scene at Platform 1, with a parcels train from Weymouth being unloaded, having been worked up by No. 7924 *Thornycroft Hall*.

[South Devon Railway Museum]

Another after-dark scene on a winter evening, showing No. 4920 *Dumbleton Hall* on 29 November 1963 on a train from Taunton. This section under the all-over roof is the original Temple Meads, dealing with all the traffic to and from the West of England and remodelled at the time of the 1892 gauge conversion. The two centre roads were provided for through traffic and light engines, etc, in the 1930s remodelling.

[South Devon Railway Museum]

No. 4940 *Ludford Hall* shunting empty stock at Temple Meads, 9 May 1959. The principal carriage siding accommodation was at Dr. Day's Bridge near Lawrence Hill and, on the west side, at Malago Vale beyond Bedminster.

[M. Mensing]

No. 6010 *King Charles I* takes water during the stop with the 7.05 a.m. Plymouth-Paddington, in February 1958. She is alongside Platform 9, which combines with No. 10 to form the longest (1366´) of the fifteen at Temple Meads.
[M. Jackson

Double-chimneyed 'Castle' No. 5031 *Totnes Castle* waiting outside Temple Meads to take over the up 'Cornishman' on 9 November 1961. This was a regular out-and-back Stafford Road (84A) turn, the same engine having worked the down 'Cornishman' south to Bristol to exchange with a 'Castle' from the far West.
[T. W. Nicholls

No. 6838 *Goodmoor Grange,* wreathed in steam, pulling out of Temple Meads with a Paignton-Manchester train, August 1963.   [W. L. Underhay]

No. 7014 *Caerhays Castle*, unkempt and workstained, gets under way with the 11.20 a.m. Newquay-Wolverhampton on a Saturday in August 1963. Her livery and BR lettering are completely hidden by grime.

[W. L. Underhay]

A contrast, five years earlier, with No. 4098 *Kidwelly Castle*, burnished and well kept by Newton Abbot shed, at the head of a Plymouth-Liverpool train. In the foreground can be seen one of the two spur roads for locomotive use at the end of this, Nos. 6 and 7, platform.

[Brian Morrison]

A nostalgic scene on the line out to Shirehampton and Avonmouth, at Clifton Down, with 0-6-0PT No. 4660 pedalling through in charge of a short freight, 7 June 1960. Opened in 1874, this line was jointly owned by the GW and LMS; it joined the main line at Narroways Hill Junction. [S. Rickard]

No. 6841 *Marlas Grange* heading an RCTS Special on a tour of the Bristol/Gloucester area on 21 July 1963, photographed at Avonmouth Docks. Beyond can be seen various of the industrial locomotives then employed in the extensive dock area.

[Derek Cross]

2-6-2T No. 6115 heading back for South Wales from Clifton Down with a lengthy excursion special from Bristol Zoo, July 1963. These trains were known among local railway men as 'Monkey Specials'.

[T. W. Nicholls]

A fitted freight of banana vans from Avonmouth heads for Pilning through New Passage Halt, behind No. 5919 *Worsley Hall* running tender-first on this single line section.

[M. Mensing]

Beneath the familiar outline of Brunel's Clifton Suspension Bridge, a four-coach train heads along the south side of the Avon gorge *en route* to Portishead behind a 45XX Class 2-6-2T on 25 May 1958. The train has just passed the former Clifton Bridge station, and along this section passes through several short tunnels cut through the limestone.

[P. J. Shoesmith]

0-6-0PT No. 7729 passes a d.m.u. at Pill whilst working the 1.00 p.m. Bristol-Portishead train, 17 February 1962. The branch out to Portishead diverged from the main line at Parson Street Junction near Malago Vale sidings and from the line to Canons Marsh goods depot at Ashton Junction

[D. H. Ballantyne]

Another scene on the former Portishead branch, with No. 7729 near Portbury Shipyard signal box and the passing loop.

[D. H. Ballantyne]

To 0-6-0PT No. 9769 fell the honour of conveying an RCTS Special on 26 September 1959 over the various goods-only lines penetrating the docks area of Bristol. The Special is seen on the now abandoned Canons Marsh branch (opposite) and also crossing Barton Road on the Avonside goods branch (left).

[R. J. Leonard]

'Star' Class No. 4056 *Princess Margaret* passing Bedminster Park with a Nottingham-Paignton Saturday extra, September 1953. She is on the main line, with the down relief line nearer to the camera; in the foreground are the up and down avoiding lines whilst on the far side are the up and down goods lines.　　　　　　[T. E. Williams]

Collett 0-6-0 No. 2203, up from St. Philips Marsh shed to help out with ECS duties on a busy day, makes a great fuss of taking stock out past Bedminster to the sidings, 27 April 1954.　　　　[T. E. Williams]

Another scene at Bedminster, with No 4978 *Westwood Hall* on the up avoiding line with a freight, 13 September 1963.

[T. W. Nicholls]

Clear of Bristol's urban limits, 2-8-0 No. 3807 nears Long Ashton with a coal train.

[R. J. Leonard]

No. 6945 *Glasfryn Hall* approaching Bedminster with a freight for Exeter on a winter day in 1963. The lines out to Parson Street Junction were quadrupled in the 1930s as part of the GWR's Bristol area improvements and extensions.

[T. W. Nicholls]

Standard 9F No. 92243 off the road at Parson Street Junction. 12 September 1963, with
No. 7907 *Hart Hall* easing past with a Plymouth train.   [T. W. Nicholls]

South of Bristol, on the line out to Frome, 24 October 1959; No. 5536 leaving Brislington with the 10.50 a.m. from Frome to Temple Meads.
[D. H. Ballantyne]

The most striking engineering feature on the route to Frome was the long sixteen-arch viaduct across the valley at Pensford, seen here with ROD 2-8-0 No. 3032 crossing on 14 March 1955 with a freight for Radstock.
[D. H. Ballantyne]

2-8-2T No. 7202 on Keynsham water troughs near Fox's Wood, with a Cardiff-Salisbury freight, 9 March 1956. Members of the 72XX Class from South Wales were regularly seen on these trains, much of the traffic being coal destined for Southern Region sidings and locomotive sheds.   [R. J. Leonard]

70

A westbound freight for Bristol passing Oldfield Park, east of Bath, headed by 2-6-0 No. 5358.
[R. E. Toop]

At the other side of Bristol on the line to Bath, No. 6979 *Helperly Hall* heads through Keynsham and Somerdale station in the spring of 1964 with a freight from Banbury.
[South Devon Railway Museum]

2-8-0 No. 2886 passing through Oldfield Park station with a South Wales coal train bound for Salisbury. By and large this was a relatively easy and level run, apart from the Severn Tunnel 'dip' and the climb from Trowbridge up through Westbury to Warminster.

[R. E. Toop]

A thirteen coach load for No. 7026 *Tenby Castle* on the 2.35 p.m. Weston-Super-Mare to Paddington, 30 June 1962. Note the reversed 'Bristolian' headboard being carried from an earlier working. Coal in the tender is chiefly notable for its absence.

[D. H. Ballantyne]

No. 5958 *Knolton Hall* leaving the castellated portal of Twerton Tunnel with a Weymouth-
Bristol stopping train, June 1962.   [D. H. Ballantyne]

No. 6909 *Frewin Hall* with a morning Cardiff-Portsmouth train near the entrance to Twerton Tunnel, 30 June 1962.

[D. H. Ballantyne]

Swindon to Bristol and back was a regular running-in duty for 'Castles' and other classes after overhaul at Swindon Works, as with No. 7015 *Carn Brea Castle* on 23 November 1957, seen running into Saltford station.

[D. H. Ballantyne]

A scene at Bath Spa in August 1963, with No. 5098 *Clifford Castle* just getting under way with a Paddington-Bristol parcels train. The unusual elevated position of the signal box here, situated above the down platform roof for sighting purposes, was a distinctive feature.

[D. H. Ballantyne]

No. 5936 *Breccles Hall* alongside the up platform at Bath Spa, 2 September 1961, with a Saturday relief from Weston-Super-Mare. The curve through the station calls for a severe speed restriction for through expresses.

[G. A. Richardson]

One of the veteran drivers from Bristol (Bath Road) shed looks back from the footplate of No. 5094 *Trelower Castle*, ready for the guard's right away, enabling his fireman to clean round the 'office' before they are off to Reading and London; 23 June 1962.

[G. A. Richardson]

A clear road ahead for No. 6974 *Bryngwyn Hall*, leaving Bath Spa with a down train in 1961.

[G. A. Richardson]

No. 6811 *Cranbourne Grange* leaving the station with an express bound for Paignton, 6 June 1959. The 'Granges' were all scrapped within a relatively short time after withdrawal and as a result none survived into the preservation era.

[S. Rickard]

No. 4908 *Broome Hall* eases away from Bath with a holiday extra in September 1961. Below, Standard 9F 2-10-0 No. 92236, pressed into service in June 1962 to work another extra up from Salisbury. [G. A. Richardson]

Carrying the incorrect headboard, reboilered 'Castle' No. 7006 *Lydford Castle* at Bath with the 9.45 Paddington to Weston-Super-Mare, 14 July 1962.

[D. H. Ballantyne]

The up side of Bath Spa in October 1958, with 'Castle' Class No. 5092 *Tresco Abbey* entering on the 10.05 a.m. local from Temple Meads.

[D. H. Ballantyne]

No.1019 *County of Merioneth* assisting No.5027 *Farleigh Castle* on a Paddington to Weston-Super-Mare train, 12 July 1959. They are emerging from Bathwick Hill Tunnel at Bath.

[D. H. Ballantyne]

Immaculate No. 3440 *City of Truro* on an RCTS enthusiasts' special bound for Bristol, pasing Sydney Gardens at Bath on 28 April 1957. This was the second main line run of this well-loved locomotive following its restoration at Swindon.   [D. H. Ballantyne]

The down 'Merchant Venturer', behind No. 6015 *King Richard III*, threads the stonelined cutting through Sydney Gardens in April 1956. This express, serving Bristol and Weston-Super-Mare, was the old-established 11.15 a.m. ex-Paddington and 4.35 p.m. up from Weston, and was given a name from June 1951 onwards.
[D. H. Ballantyne]

During the Bath Festival in 1959, the 9.05 a.m. Paddington to Bristol carried a large commemorative headboard, as seen here on No. 6009 *King Charles II* arriving at Bath Spa on 13 June.

[D. H. Ballantyne]

The replacement of Brunel's skew bridge at Bath in 1959 after 117 years of service necessitated a great deal of heavy engineering work and wrong line working. Here, No. 6932 *Burwarton Hall* comes in dead slow over the down line with a morning Cardiff-Portsmouth train on 25 October.

[D. H. Ballantyne]

The 5.35 p.m. Salisbury-Cardiff train was a regular 'Hall' turn, as witness No. 6935 *Browsholme Hall*, near Hampton Row at Bath on a July evening in 1962. The brick and stone wall that is such a feature here (and through Sydney Gardens) retains the canal running parallel above.　　　　　　　　　[D. H. Ballantyne]

On a day in April 1960, No. 5042 *Winchester Castle* passing milepost 105.111 with the down 'Merchant Venturer'. A single maroon LM region coach at the end of the train spoils the otherwise harmonious appearance of its chocolate-and-cream livery.

[D. H. Ballantyne]

The 5.20 p.m. Weymouth to Bristol stopping train behind No. 5924 *Dinton Hall* passing Bathampton goods loop, 6 July 1962. Most South Wales to Salisbury freights took water here, before diverging from the main line at the junction just east of Bathampton station.

[D. H. Ballantyne]

'Castle' Class No. 5090 *Neath Abbey* approaching Bathampton station with the 10.30 a.m. Cardiff-Portsmouth train, 19 August 1958. One of Bath Road's 24 or so allocated 'Castles' in the 1950s, *Neath Abbey* was withdrawn in 1962.

[D. H. Ballantyne]

A gentle run down to Bristol and back was an ideal running-in turn after overhaul at Swindon, the 10.15 a.m. from there to Temple Meads being frequently headed in this way. Here, No. 6850 *Cleeve Grange* restarts this train from Bathampton in August 1958, in pristine condition and displaying an 83D (Laira) shedplate.   [D. H. Ballantyne]

No. 7034 *Ince Castle* near little-used Bathford Halt, east of Bathampton, with a down express to Bristol. [R. E. Toop]

A 'Hall' at speed; No. 4936 *Kinlet Hall* passing MP 105 near Bathampton with an up express
in July 1962.
[D. H. Ballantyne]

On a cold March morning in 1961, No. 5023 *Brecon Castle* raises a plume of steam and smoke as she draws away from Mill Lane Halt with the 6.40 a.m. Bristol-Swindon local.

[D. H. Ballantyne]

No. 4975 *Umberslade Hall* with a Bristol-Paddington parcels train heads out of Middle Hill Tunnel towards Mill Lane Halt and Box Tunnel, 12 May 1962. The gradient here, after the near-level run from Temple Meads, is 1 in 120 and sharpens to 1 in 100 for the next two miles.

[G. A. Richardson]

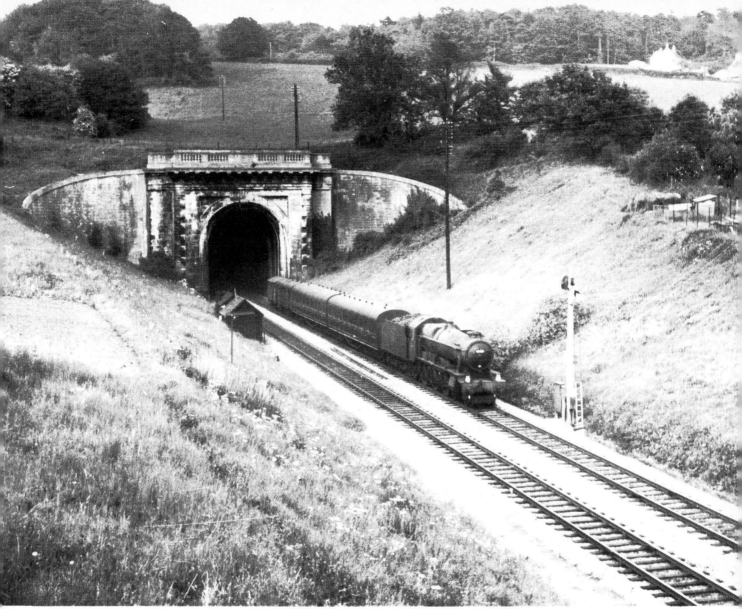

No. 1028 *County of Warwick* in the cutting by Box Tunnel, 6 June 1962, with a Swindon-Bristol train. The tunnel, 1 mile 1452 yards long, is on a gradient of 1 in 100 for eastbound trains and was the load limiting factor on the Bristol-Paddington run. It is dead straight and despite its length can be seen through from end to end.   [T. W. Nicholls]

Overleaf: No. 5093 *Upton Castle* emerging from the classically-sculptured portal of Box Tunnel with the down 'Bristolian', 3 August 1956, diverted on this occasion via Bath rather than the Badminton route usual up to 1958.   [T. E. Williams]